# ARE YOU READY

# FOR MANAGEMENT?

## A SIMPLE GUIDE TO MEASURING YOUR SKILLS

By Roberta E. Elliott Speight

Are You Ready For Management?
A SIMPLE GUIDE TO MEASURING YOUR SKILLS

ISBN: 13: 978-1481155397

# Introduction

This booklet, a short extension of my training management class, it is to be used as a reference. Are you ready for management training is conducted in government training programs across the United States, as well as private companies? *Are You Ready for Management* will provide those who are considering a managerial position with a closer look at what it is to be a leader and what key things will make them successful when dealing with others.

This booklet can also serve as a quick refresher for those who are currently in managerial positions with one to two years of experiences.

The words leadership and management will be used interchangeably throughout the booklet.

# Table of Contents

# WHAT IS

# LEADERSHIP?

### What is leadership?

Leadership is part of the process of social influence in which one person enlists the aid and support of others in the accomplishment of a common task. Leadership is a skill that can be learned or that one may be born with.

### What is a manager?

A manager is a person who has control of or gives direction to a business or institution, or to any of its parts, divisions or phases. People who direct, manage and/or organize are managers.

### Questions to ponder before taking a leadership position

Do you have the skills to be a leader?

_____

What qualities of leadership do you possess?

_____

What makes you a good leader?

_____

Are you a good communicator?

_____

Do you know when and how to be assertive?

_____

Do you know how to motivate your team?

_____

Are you a good follower (student)?

_____

**NOTES**

# SKILLS OF A
# LEADER

**Do you possess and use the following leadership skills?**

Planning: Do you have the ability to plan ahead and always have a back-up plan?

Diagnosing the problem: Are you able to diagnose the problem, step back and look at the whole picture before finding a solution that can help all parties?

Providing help: Are you able or willing to provide help or direction to someone?

Organizing meetings: Can you organize a meeting or act as a good facilitator?

Encouraging others: Can you inspire?

Showing patience: Do you demonstrate patience with others when looking for the solution to a problem?

Setting goals: Do you set personal goals and professional goals for yourself?

Making decisions: Can you make a decision and feel confident that it is the right one?

Finding solutions: Do you seek outside sources for solutions by doing such things as consulting with other departments, holding brain-storming sessions or check with other similar companies?

Building skills: Do you continue to build on your skills and teach others as you learn?

Team-building: Are you able to build an effective team that will trust you?

Getting assistance: Do you seek help by participating in other organizations, such as American Society of Association Executives (ASAE), or Society for Human Resource Management (SHRM)?

Being a role model: Are you a role model in your organization?

## What Skills Do You Have?

As a leader, it is imperative to be able to do the following:

Clarify and express my values and beliefs.

Inspire the shared vision.

Encourage thinking outside the box.

Understand the budget and the planning process.

Engage in goal-setting.

Develop and implement action plans.

**NOTES**

# TYPES OF
# LEADERSHIP

## Types of Leadership

Understanding the types of leadership you have can help you work and communicate better with others, both professionally and personally. (As you read the descriptions that follow, be honest with yourself.)

## Charismatic Leadership

Creating a self-image so powerful that people are naturally drawn to you.

Charismatic leaders gather followers through their personality and charm, rather than any aggressive show of external power or authority.

## Participant Leadership (Working Together)

The democratic leadership style is encourages employees to be a part of the decision-making. The democratic manager keeps his or her employees informed about everything that affects their work and shares decision-making and problem-solving responsibilities.

## Delegate (You Figure It Out!) Leadership

This is hands-off leadership, also known as the "hands-off style", because the leader allows group members to make decisions. The manager provides little or no direction and gives employees as much freedom as possible.

**Bureaucratic (By-the-Book) Leadership**

The manager manages "by the book." Everything must be done according to procedure or policy. There is no room for comprise.

**Authoritarian (Bossy) Leadership**

Authoritarian leadership is an extreme form of transactional leadership. The leader has absolute power over his or her employees or team. Employees and team members have little opportunity to make suggestions, even if they would be in the team or organization's best interest.

Most people resent being treated in this way, and therefore, autocratic leadership usually leads to high levels of absenteeism and frequent staff turnover. For certain routine

14

or unskilled jobs, where the advantages of control outweigh the disadvantages, this style can be effective.

**Laissez-faire (You Got This!) Leadership**

This French phrase means "let it be." It is used to describe an approach in which the leader leaves his or her colleagues to get on with their work in their own way. It can be effective if the leader monitors what is being achieved and communicates this to his or her team regularly.

**NOTES**

# THE FIVE BASES
# OF POWER

## Five Bases of Power

Five bases of power were identified by French and Raven in 1960, and this provided the groundwork for most discussions of power and authority in the latter half of the twentieth century. These five types of power are coercive, legitimate, reward, referent and expert. Power in leadership can be manifested through one or more of these bases of power.

## Coercive Power

Coercive power lies in the ability of a manager to force an employee to comply with an order through the threat of punishment. Coercive power typically leads to short-term compliance, but in the long-run produces dysfunctional behavior.

Coercion reduces the employee's satisfaction with his or her job, leading to lack of commitment and general employee withdrawal.

## Legitimate Power

Legitimate power rests in the belief among employees that their manager has the right to give orders based on his or her position. For example, at the scene of a crime, people usually comply with the orders of a uniformed police officer based simply on their shared belief that he or she has the predetermined authority to give such orders. In a corporate setting, employees comply with the orders of a manager who relies on legitimate power, based on his position in the organizational hierarchy. Yet, although employees may comply based on legitimate power, they may not feel a sense of commitment to or spirit of cooperation in the company.

## Reward Power

Reward power, as the name implies, is based on the ability of a manager to give some sort of reward to employees. These rewards can range from monetary compensation to improved work schedules. Reward power may not need monetary or other tangible compensation to work when managers can convey various intangible benefits as rewards.

## Referent Power (Personal Power)

Referent power derives from an employee's respect for a manager and desire to identify with or emulate him or her. Using referent power, the manager leads by example. Referent power rests heavily on trust. It often influences employees who may not be particularly aware that they are modeling their behavior on that of the manager and using what they presume he or she would do in a particular situation as a point of reference.

**Personal Power**

Personal Power is the ability or power to attract others to build strong and interpersonal relationships to create and build an alliance of loyalty.

**Expert Power**

Expert power rests on the belief of employees that an individual has a particularly high level of knowledge or a highly specialized skill set. Managers may be the expert authority based on the perception of their greater knowledge of the tasks at hand than their employees have.

Ask yourself the following:

- **Which, if any, of the leadership powers do you exercise?**
- **Do you exercise these same powers in your personal life—with your spouse, children or friends?**
- **How does this power affect your work relationships and personal life?**
- **Do you think you could be flexible and change your leadership skills?**

**NOTES**

# KNOWING YOUR COMMUNICATION SKILLS

### Knowing Your Communication Skills

At work we come across many different types of personalities. Someone once asked me what was my favorite and least favorite part of my job. My reply was, "The many different personalities, and the many different personalities."

We all are different, coming from different cultures, social backgrounds and life experiences. In order to get the results you are striving for as a leader, you must understand a little about the people who work with you: What motivates them? What types of personality do they have? What are their goals? Then help them find the inner strength and positive energy to succeed. You might be the only person who has ever invested in them.

Leaders should never degrade or belittle employees in public. Always stop negative behavior in a professional manner. Give yourself time to reflect and write notes about an incident before calling an employee into your office. Never let more than 24 hours passed before addressing or following up on an issue. Remember to know the personality type that you are addressing. You may need a third party to help facilitate or be a witness to the meeting.

**Identify Essential Communication Skills**

Be honest and rate yourself.

1 = Weak

2 = Not consistent

3 = Good but needs improvement

4 = Strong Point

Assertiveness

_____

Conflict management

_____

Ability to realize resolutions

_____

Ability to listen well

_____

Ability to comprehend written and verbal communication

_____

Ability to think clearly

_____

Ability to interpret nonverbal cues

_____

Ability to respect others

_____

Ability to follow directions

_____

Ability to train others

_____

## NOTES

# ALPHA DOG

# EMPLOYEES

**Alpha Dog Employees**

Within each cluster or on each level of an organization there is an Alpha Dog—the leader of the pack. The Alpha Dog can set the tone of your department and lead the rest of the employees to follow his or her type of thinking. Some alpha behavior can be borderline bullying. This person might display Authoritarian Leadership.

Many mid-level employees find it hard to submit to the ideas of the Alpha Dog and will usually play by their own rules until caught. Your support staff—the "honey bee workers"— are dedicated workers, but there is always one alpha in the group. This is because much of the time we hire people that are like ourselves, rather than thinking outside the box and looking for something unique that a person can bring to the organization. Sometimes, Alpha Dog behavior is more noticeable in the worker bee because of his or her communication across departments with other worker bees in order to complete a task. At the worker bee level, the Alpha Dog runs around barking all the time. This is the one who creates negativity in the environment, no matter what is presented. Although the majority will not agree with him, others will join the Alpha Dog as long as he or she continues to bark loudly and long enough.

For a new manager this behavior is hard to stop because it has been allowed to continue long enough to be deemed acceptable. However, this is where you the leader, need to use the Alpha Dog to your advantage—to use his or her abilities to complete special projects. Make the Alpha Dog feel important. Once you get him or her working with you instead of against you, everyone else who runs with the Alpha Dog will soon follow. The atmosphere of the work place will be more positive than negative. (Alpha dog behavior is discussed more in the training class.)

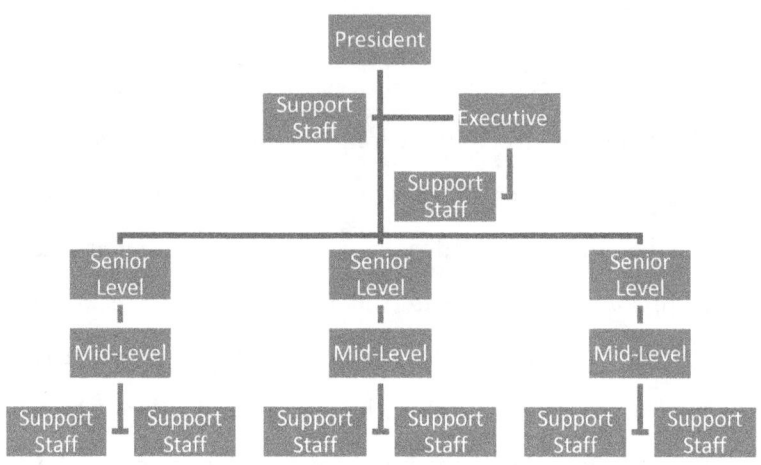

Remember! When dealing with strong or dominant personalities, you need to adjust your style of leadership dealing with them. My point is that if you have two authoritarian individuals, there will certain be a stand-off of power. You are the leader and you must be able to change your style to deal with the individuals.

Learn to use the strength of an employee's dominant personality. Is he/she an organizer, trainer, thinker or logic-oriented person? Use people's strengths to your advantage and help them drive their strength to become a positive influence for the organization.

**NOTES**

# WHAT IS CONFLICT?

**Conflict**

What is conflict? Conflict occurs when your values, perspectives and opinions are contradictory to those of other people and they haven't been aligned or reconciled. Every conflict is different and thus should be handled differently.

Conflict is a good thing. Why do I say this?

Conflict brings up issues and concerns that others may have but will not voice, giving the leader the chance to resolve them.

It brings out many points of views that may be different yet in some ways the same. This may help you resolve issues.

People are more relaxed when they are motivated and able or willing to give their opinion. (Sometimes this happens in a manner that is not particularly inviting.)

Why is conflict frowned upon? Conflict is frowned upon because it is usually not managed well, and this results in problems:

It becomes a stumbling block to productivity in the workplace.

It crushes the morale in the workplace.

It causes employees to act inappropriately in the workplace.

**Here are some simple conflict resolutions**

Don't allow the situation to escalate. Take a few minutes to walk away from the situation and come back when everyone has cooled off.

Stay focused on the current issue—not on what happened in the past.

Respect the opinions of others. You may not agree with someone, but this does not give you the right to reject what he or she is saying without considering it.

Don't point the finger of blame.

Don't assume that you know what the other person is thinking or feeling about a situation.

Focus on the common thread of the problem, not on uncommon issues

Do not bring up past behavior that was not addressed previously just to make a point about the current situation.

Conflict only becomes ugly when management does not address an issue within 24 hours of its occurrence.

Also, when the leader is not experienced enough, the conflict spreads through the organization. Then, while you are trying to figure out how to resolve the conflict, fact and fiction become blurred, and this makes the solution harder to achieve.

**Conflict Management**

Conflict management requires communication skills, problem-solving abilities and experience combined with counseling techniques in order to diffuse the tension and come to a resolution that works for both parties.

# PITFALLS OF
# MANAGEMENT

## Pitfalls of Management that Cause Conflict in the Workplace

Pitfalls that managers should avoid include the following:

Poor communication or lack of communication

Speaking about an employee to other employees

Being inconsistent or not informed

Passing blame to someone

Not following through on decisions

Not understanding the jobs of subordinates

37

Not understanding who is responsible for which job (who does what)

Making changes and decisions that shock employees

Giving two or more employees the same title but different job requirements

Not having the same expectation of all employees

Having a Human Relations (HR) department with unskilled employees

Not having a balance of knowledge and experience

Having insufficient managerial training

Leaders are obligated to train and invest in themselves and others. When we move up the ladder in the corporate world, our commitment is to touch and make a difference in the lives others. An employee who has been well invested in is a happy and productive one.

**NOTES**

Are you ready to take on the challenge of investing in yourself and others? Are you ready for management?

To learn more or to arrange for Miss Bert to visit your facility to train your staff, contact her at missbert.com or robertaespeight@yahoo.com.

**References:**

McNamara, Carter, MBA, PhD. *Basics of Conflict Management Adapted from the Field Guide to Leadership and Supervision.* Authenticity Consulting, LLC. 1997-2008.

French, J. P. R. Jr., and Raven, B.. "The bases of social power." D. Cartwright and A. Zander (eds.), *Group Dynamics* (pp. 607-623). New York: Harper and Row. 1960.

http://www.dictionary.com

www.ingramcontent.com/pod-product-compliance
Lightning Source LLC
Chambersburg PA
CBHW051301170526
45165CB00004B/1805